MW00825152

ANGEL IN A FOXHOLE
SMOKY THE THERAPY DOG

A Coloring Book for All Ages

Written by Dave Tabar
Illustrated by Samantha Williams

Special thanks to William A. Wynne

© 2019 Studio A Films LLC
All Rights Reserved
ISBN 978-1-54395-966-6

Happy Engagement!

Friends for Life

Smoky's in the Army now!

Bill goes on a combat mission

Smoky loves to have fun!

Smoky follows orders to protect lives

Nurse takes Smoky on rounds

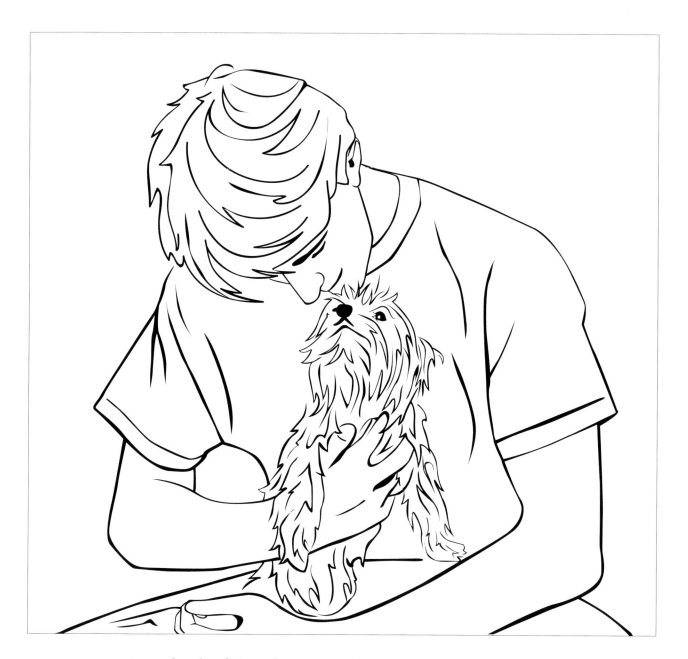

Smoky befriends wounded and lonely soldiers

Mascot of the Southwest Pacific

Blue Ribbons for Smoky!

Margie is devoted to Bill

Bill and Smoky entertain on live television post-war

Smoky performs on the tight-wire

"Margie"

"Ain't No Mystery" Margie enjoys listening to jazz